Classical Organ Music 2

from the death of J. S. Bach to the advent of Mendel
Edited in three volumes by Robin Langley

Volume 2   With pedals

Oxford University Press, Walton Street, Oxford OX2 6DP, England
Oxford University Press, 200 Madison Avenue, New York, NY 10016, USA

The cover design incorporates a photograph of the organ in the Abteikirche, Amorbach.

Music Department
OXFORD UNIVERSITY PRESS
Oxford and New York

PREFACE

The solo organ repertoire from the Classical and early Romantic period, bounded roughly by the death of J. S. Bach in 1750 and the publication of the major organ works of Mendelssohn in 1837–45, is possibly the least explored sector of one of the richest three-quarters of a century in musical history. It was a period of war, from the militarism of Frederick the Great to Napoleon, social change, from the secularization of the monasteries to the French Revolution, and musical change, from late-Baroque textures sympathetic to the mechanism of the organ as then established to the kaleidoscopic colours and dynamics of the early nineteenth century which presaged, and, in the present period, outgrew the pace of development towards that flexibility demanded by the Romantic style.

That these conditions, while fostering other branches of the repertory,[1] militated against that of the organ in its established environment, the Church, may be amply seen from the writings of Burney[2] near the beginning of the period, and Holmes[3] and Novello[4] near the end. The organ regularly took a subsidiary role, acting as continuo to an increasing tradition of orchestrally accompanied service music; it was regularly replaced by other instruments (the serpent or other wind instruments persisted in France throughout the period); it remained unused as the gallery in which it was placed was often too small to accommodate an orchestra;[5] this in turn often displaced the organ prelude and postlude by symphonic music.[6] Even if there were no orchestra, there was often no possibility of extended organ music as many instruments, especially the larger ones, were in chronic disrepair through war damage and neglect. As late as 1823, Mendelssohn wrote bleakly from Breslau: 'Then he showed me the inside of the organ itself. Shot and shell have struck many pipes so they are useless'.[7] Burney and Novello provide examples of instruments where the choruses were incomplete and most of the solo stops unplayable, and all three writers are constant in their complaint at the lack of tuning.

Small wonder that with the common state of instruments, the sparse opportunity for extended playing, and the increasing secularization of style, the majority of organists took refuge in extemporization, or pillage of the piano repertoire—the lesser of them with risible results.[8] The development of an idiomatic organ style to suit changing needs was delayed and music specifically composed for solo organ a rarity. If the contribution of England, the Iberian peninsula, and (to some extent) Italy was insulated from these conditions, that of the single great composer of the period with a life-long interest in and virtuosic command of the organ, Mozart, was not. Given his stature, some justification is needed for the inclusion of solo organ music by him here.

Mozart played an organ concerto at Ranelagh in 1764 and two years later an Amsterdam concert notice promised that 'the boy will play on the organ his own capricci'.[9] These (K.32a, composed 1765–6) are now lost, although they existed in 1799–1800, and it is just possible that K.72a (see Vol. 1, p. 14) was one of them.[10] For K.383a (see Vol. 3, p. 2), Mozart's letter to his sister of 20 April 1782 is illuminating: 'My dear Constanze is really the cause of this fugue's coming into the world . . . as she has often heard me play fugues out of my head, she asked me if I had ever written any down, and when I said I had not, she scolded me roundly for not recording some of my compositions in this most artistic and beautiful of all musical forms'.[11] It is clear that, without this stimulus, which lasted in sporadic form only during his intense contrapuntal studies of 1782–3, Mozart had relied, and was to continue to rely, on improvisation as the main source of his own solo organ repertoire.[12] 'Mozart's *extempore* playing was so exquisitely regular and symmetrical in design, that it was impossible for judges who heard him not to imagine that the whole had been written before'.[13] This of course reflects Mozart's methods of composition, in which writing down was merely the final chore in the process,[14] and it is largely a matter of chance that with one exception[15] he chose to commit to paper in an allied medium some music putatively conceived for organ.

For K.385e (see Vol. 2, p. 14), written out as the second movement of a violin and piano sonata, the internal evidence is strong. Only three times does the music exceed the stretch of two hands, necessitating the entry of the pedals, and each of them underlines a musical point. Two of these (bb. 21 and 51) comprise the only entries of the same derivation of the countersubject, the third (b. 38), the only appearance of a non-fugal harmonic bass figure well within the practice and pedal technique of the time.[16] Note too the particularly idiomatic shape for pedals of the fugue subject of K.383a and the opportunity to use them sparingly on two occasions, each, again, to underline a musical point: the only occurrence of the theme in augmentation (which Mozart introduces in the bass rather than any other part), and the last entry of the subject to the final cadence.[17] K.540 (see Vol. 3, p. 14) is stylistically very close to the florid cantabile pieces in Knecht's *Neue Vollständige Sammlung . . . für geübtere und ungeübtere Klavier und Orgel Spieler*[18] (issued in five volumes to 1812),

[1] E.g. the orchestrally accompanied concerto (by such as Corrette, C. P. E. Bach, M. and J. Haydn, Brixi, Vanhal, Soler, and the English school), works for two, three, and four organs (by Luchinetti, Cherubini, and the Iberian school), and domestic music for house organ (the sonatas of Soler, Cirri, and C. P. E. Bach among others).

[2] Charles Burney, *The Present State of Music in France and Italy; . . . Germany, the Netherlands, and United Provinces* (London, 1773); Charles Burney, ed. H. Edmund Poole, *Music, Men, and Manners in France and Italy 1770* (London, 1969), *passim*.

[3] [Edward Holmes], *A Ramble among the Musicians of Germany* (London, 1828), *passim*.

[4] [Vincent Novello], transcr. N. M. di Marignano, ed. Rosemary Hughes, *A Mozart Pilgrimage being the Travel Diaries of Vincent and Mary Novello in the year 1829* (London, 1955), *passim*.

[5] In such cases a small chamber organ placed near the orchestra became usual; Mozart's Epistle Sonatas are among the fruits of this practice.

[6] Novello, op. cit., pp. 290–1 instances particularly Haydn's Symphony No. 99 and Overture *Armida*.

[7] Sebastian Hensel, *The Mendelssohn Family* (London, 1881), vol. 1, p. 119.

[8] Edward Holmes, op. cit., p. 31 and Felix Mendelssohn, ed. G.

[9] D. F. Scheurleer, *Het Musikleven in Nederland* ('s Gravenhage, 1909), p. 327.

[10] The upper compass to d''', common enough on Dutch organs but regularly a tone lower in Italy at this period, supports this view.
 Its source is the dalla Rosa portrait executed on 6–7 January 1770 at which time Mozart played the organ at Rovereto, near Verona. Only the first page is depicted (with less than the usual painterly inaccuracy), hence the editorial completion.

[11] Emily Anderson, *The Letters of Mozart and his family* (London, 1985/3), p. 801.

[12] K.300g (1777) and Lehmann's unfinished transcription of an improvisation played in the Strahov Church, Prague, K.528a (1787) (see Alfred Ebert, '*Eine freie Phantasie Mozarts*' in *Die Musik X*, 1 (1910), p. 106) are compositions in both the free and imitative styles which have survived in part.

[13] Edward Holmes, op. cit., p. 134, quoting the Abbé Stadler.

[14] 'I composed the fugue first and wrote it down while I was thinking out the prelude [K.383a]' (Emily Anderson, op. cit., p. 800).

[15] The 16-bar fragment K.383d (1782), headed 'Thema Man[ualiter]', probably designed as an *aide-memoire* upon which to improvise a set of variations. For a near-contemporary set in the same genre, see J. H. Knecht, *Vollständige Orgelschule* (Leipzig, 1795–8), II Abteilung, p. 53.

[16] Conversely, the musical clock pieces K.594, 608, and 616, at present the only Mozart 'organ-works' in the regular repertoire, all exceed the practical possibilities of organs and organists of late eighteenth-century Hapsburg Europe in both keyboard and pedal range and technique.

[17] It should be remembered that Mozart was not only familiar with the problems of short-octave pedal-boards (letter to his father from Augsburg 17 October 1777; Emily Anderson, op. cit., p. 329), but that in 1785 he 'had a large fortepiano pedal [keyboard, with strings at 16' pitch] made, which stands under the instrument' (Emily Anderson, op. cit., p. 889) which he used regularly when performing his piano concertos in public.

[18] Note the option for both instruments, even though the former is

and forms part of a tradition from Eberlin, Salzburg court organist in Mozart's youth, to Hummel and Czerny (see Vol. 2, pp. 28 and 30). Knecht's own *Vorspiel mit volgriffigen Accorden und untermischten Sprungen* (No. 3 in Volume 2 of the above collection) provides a near identical thematic concordance with bars 56–7 and other features in K.383*a*, while the fourth of Albrechtsberger's *Six Preludes et Fugues pour l'Orgue ou Pianoforte . . . Oeuvre 15* (Vienna, c.1795), constitutes the prime example of a piece in similarly brilliant arpeggiesque style published in that curious period notation, suitable to neither instrument as it stands, but serving as a framework for extempore adaptation to the idiom of whichever is being played at the time.

It is also Knecht[19] who provides the solution to the final problem:

The Adept Use of the Pedals. Precis: The way the Pedal is to be employed, *as it is very seldom notated* (*and frequently not at all*); how the ordinary bass in organ *and other pieces* is to be supported and accompanied by the pedals . . . The pedal can, depending on the kind of piece it is, be used in three ways: (*i*) sparingly, (*ii*) following, on the whole, the manual bass, (*iii*) quite on its own, or diverging from the manual bass. The sparing use of the pedal is mainly employed in pleasant and cantabile pieces where it is sufficient to point the single main notes in order not to darken the melody or finely-wrought accompaniment figure through a continuous humming in the bass . . . one only plays with the pedal a pointing-in [cf. K.540] of the first note of the undulating accompaniment . . . A knowledge of harmony . . . to pick out the main notes of a running bass (as distinct from subsidiary or passing notes) [cf. K.383*a*, and 385*e*] and good musical taste and judgement must also contribute its part if the pedal accompaniment is to be appropriate to the character of the piece . . . If passages too fast or difficult occur in a piece (irrespective of its type or character) play with the pedal only the first note (which anyway usually turns out to be the main one [harmonically]), or you can simplify the runs in the pedal by means of long notes [cf. K.383*a*] . . . In the course of a piece, if Tenor, Alto, and Soprano contrapuntal lines occur (not only in fugues but also in other pieces), it is natural that when the ordinary [manual] Bass is silent, the pedals should be too. However, such contrapuntal sections are excluded when both hands have so much to do that the pedal has to help out with the ordinary bass [cf. K.385*e*] . . . In the *gallant* or brilliant manner of organ playing [cf. Fantasy K.383*a*], where the right and left hands are partly together and partly in dialogue, and also in fast and staccato fashion, the pedal can be played in three ways: 1) when the fingers of both hands are at top speed, the pedal points

the main notes giving an organ-like fullness, without which the texture would sound thin; 2) play the main notes of such fast figuration staccato and hold the final one (at the end of a phrase) longer, to give more strength and emphasis; 3) in the most *gallant* organ pieces, employ, on the one hand, an isolated staccato pedal note only occasionally, and, on the other, after a long pedal rest produce a number of consecutive notes reinforcing the main line of the [manual] bass . . . At a concluding cadence the pedal can make two distinctive alternative contributions, as follows . . . it can hold down the dominant while both hands play either delicately and quickly or imitatively and contrapuntally [cf. editorial conclusion to K.385*e*]; or it can enter quickly, literally just before the final note . . . The last note, the tonic, can (though more rarely) also be held on while the hands are playing delicately or contrapuntally. But it will sound far better, and give in the church a nicer after-echo, if one cuts off the final note in both manuals and pedals [Curiously, both Burney and Novello (op. cit.) criticize this effect as unsatisfactory, at least to English ears] . . . While one is holding full chords with both hands with both manuals coupled together and playing simultaneously broken chords with the pedals, this way of using the pedal produces on the whole a particularly good effect [See M. G. Fischer's *Nachspiel V*, Vol. 3, p. 19].

Fischer was the first important influence on the formulation of an idiomatic early nineteenth-century organ style as synthesized by Mendelssohn; his *Choralbuch* (1821) was the subject of an intensive course of study between Mendelssohn and his teacher, Zelter. Samuel Wesley was the second, and his sequence of large-scale voluntaries in several movements (particularly Opus 6), with which Mendelssohn was familiar from his first London visit in 1829, clearly presaged the structure of his organ sonatas. The third influence, as though the previous three-quarters of a century of organ music had never been, was J. S. Bach.

I am grateful to Maestro Floriano Balestro and Dr Bohumil Geist for assistance during research in Italy and Czechoslovakia, to Elisabeth von Petersdorff for providing the translation from Knecht's *Orgelschule*, to the librarians and staff of the Deutsche Staatsbibliothek, Berlin, the British Library and Royal College of Music, London, the National Library, Madrid, the Bibliothèque Nationale and Bibliothèque Municipale de Versailles, Paris, the National and Conservatoire Libraries, Prague, the Mozarteum, Salzburg, and the Gesellschaft der Musikfreunde, Vienna, for provision of access to and material from their holdings, and to my publishers for their patience while I pursued my researches into this fascinating subject.

[19] J. H. Knecht, *Vollständige Orgelschule* (Leipzig, 1795–8), I Abteilung, pp. 81–6; the italics are editorial. The copious music examples, omitted here for reasons of space, are illustrative of the editorial method employed in the reconstruction of idiomatic pedal parts for the present edition.

Robin Langley
Bayswater, 1986

EDITORIAL METHOD

All notes, rests, and accidentals printed small, all material in square brackets, crossed slurs and ties, angle brackets indicating hand distribution, rhythmic indications and notation on small staves above the main text, are editorial. Material in round brackets is from secondary sources; original texts in C clefs are transposed to treble or bass as appropriate. With the exception of Mozart, where *urtexts* are readily accessible, all deviations from original texts are noted in the Critical Commentary, together with notes on the individual pieces as appropriate.

CRITICAL COMMENTARY

1 For *voce umana*, see Vol. 1, no. 2. A rare later eighteenth-century example of the genre essayed in Zipoli's *Sonate d'Intavolatura per Organo* (Rome, 1716). The pedals, permanently coupled to the manual and used as a third hand, had little individual character, possessing perhaps soft 16' tone for the *upper* octave only of their compass (usually *C–e*, with or without short octave). Often constructed as slats at 45 degrees to the case front, they precluded all but the most stately movement from note to note.

2 The Spanish tripartite *tiento*, finely wrought here in late Classical harmonic terms, used the standard two manuals (*Órgano Grande* and *Cadireta*) each with full chorus, separately for the exposition of the two themes, and coupled for their combination in the final section. The relevance of the two parallel sets of pedal keys (or studs) commonly found in Spain, accommodating two sets of supportive dynamic levels, can be clearly seen.
33 soprano note 1 *^{c}*/ 124 soprano note 5 *d''*/ 125 tenor note 4 *g*/ 126 alto note 4 *c''*/ 137 tenor note 5 down stem *^{c}* for bass omitted/ 206 *despacio*=slow, ie. *adagio* in the sense of inviting a cadenza

3a A number of Oley's chorale preludes are provided, like this one, with doubling instrumental parts, in this case 2 flutes, oboe, bassoon, and 2 horns. The texture of the organ parts with or without accompaniment is essentially the same.
6, 34 soprano note 4 *d''^{c}*, *g''^{q}* from oboe part

3b See Vol. 1, no. 13b for another setting of this chorale by the same composer.

4 28 note 2–29 note 6 alto *8ve* higher/ 58 note 3: Mozart left this fugue unfinished; the ending is editorial/ 64 tenor note 2: this kind of clash occurs elsewhere in Mozart's contrapuntal writing; those who prefer to avoid it may substitute *c'* or *b'*

6 *Voluntary XII* in the original edition comprises an introductory Adagio for diapasons, a movement with trumpet stop, and a March for full organ, all in C minor. Then follows, without title, the Introduction and Fugue presented here. Musically the two sequences of movements, in C minor and C major, are each self-sufficient. The avoidance of the number 13 would appear to be the only reason for treating the two sequences as a single piece hitherto. Much of the bass line is written in octaves, taking advantage of the old English manual compass downward to *G'*; the lower octaves are here omitted in the following passages: 1 note 1–note 3, 6 note 2–10 note 1, 38–43 note 1, 57–64 note 1, 67–74 note 1, 119–127 note 2, 136–141 note 1, 164–169 note 1, 171 note 1–173 note 1, 175–182, 201–212, 218 note 2–227. The accents in bars 7–8 will be achieved by timing.
149 l.h. notes 3–4 downstems omitted

7a For a composer held in such high regard in his own time, it is telling that Hummel's organ music remained nonetheless in MS. The two staves of this 'Trioschenspiel' are marked 'Vox hum' [r.h.] and 'Flöten Reg:' [l.h. and ped.]. However the distribution between the hands is unsatisfactory if these directions are followed, and the exact meaning unclear. Editorial indications for changes of registration are provided.
34 l.h. note 1 *c'^{q}* omitted; the possibility that this is a pedal entry on *E♭* in the (understood) bass clef is rejected/ 36 alto note 3 *^{c}*/ 67–9 ped. intended for a resonant acoustic

CLASSICAL ORGAN MUSIC

Volume 2

1. [TOCCATA per l'] ELEVAZIONE

Museo Correr, Venice
MS Busta 49–70

Giuseppe PAOLUCCI
(1726–76)

Printed in Great Britain

OXFORD UNIVERSITY PRESS, MUSIC DEPARTMENT, WALTON STREET, OXFORD OX2 6DP

2. INTENTO [TRIPLA]

*Biblioteca Nacional,
Madrid. MS Fondo
Barbieri G.5a.23*

José LIDON
(1746–1827)

[**Vivace maestoso**]

[Ped.]

* An *ad libitum* expansion of the cadence, such as the following, is permitted here:

(Ped.)

3. [TWO CHORALE PRELUDES]

a. Ich hab in Gottes Herz und Sinn

*Variirte Choräle für die
Orgel...3 Teil, F.J. Ernst,
Quedlinburg, 1791.*

Johann Christoph OLEY
(1738–89)

b. Nun danket alle Gott

Choralvorspiele und Orgelstücke
verschiedener Art ... Erstes Heft
... Hofmeister, Leipzig [1825]

H. W. TAUSCHER
(*fl. c.* 1825)

[**Allegretto**]

4. FUGUE

W. A. MOZART
(1756–91)

K. 385e [*1782*]

Allegro moderato

5. TRIO II

*Sechs Trios für die Orgel,
...dem Herrn Kapellmeister
Karl Philipp Emanuel Bach
...zugeeignet ... Breitkopf,
Dresden und Leipzig, 1787.*

Johann Ernst REMBT
(1749–1810)

Etwas lebhaft [Poco vivace ma andante]

6. [VOLUNTARY XIII]

*Twelve Voluntaries for the
Organ or Piano forte...
Clementi, London [1805].*

William RUSSELL
(1777–1813)

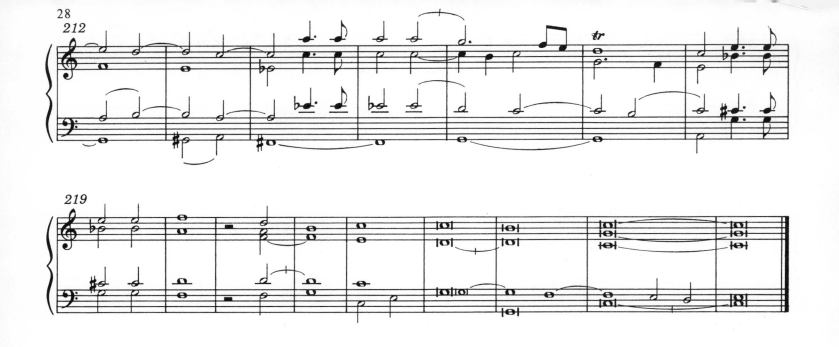

7. [TWO ARIAS]

a.

Johann Nepomuk HUMMEL
(1778–1837)

b.

20 Short Voluntaries
...Op. 698. R. Cocks & Co.,
London [1842]. No. 18

Carl CZERNY
(1791–1857)

Lento cantabile